Don't Forget Me

Kayla Jarmon

Illustrations

PIPER MIRÚ

Dedication

This book is dedicated to Mothers
and exists for God's glory.

All proceeds go to God's Kingdom purposes.

I'm Thankful

- For the Lord. Thank you for nudging me into writing books and for giving me the stories to write. My prayer is that they bring you glory.
- For Emet. God used you to inspire me to write books. Even from your mother's womb. And you still inspire me every day!
- For my husband, sons, and daughter-in-love. You have been a constant source of help in many ways.
- For Piper. I was waiting for you, and in God's timing, he brought you near. Your illustrations move me!
- For Piper's mother, my friend, Jen. Thank you for striving with me in putting this book together.
- For Steve. Your help was invaluable. We and the world are the recipients of your tireless efforts.
- For Mom and Dad. Your love of story-telling was contagious!
- For Valerie Scott. God ordained our friendship and giftings.
- For Sarah F. Kremer. Thank you for your valuable input about delivery rooms. You helped me give closure the way I desired.
- For Ann. Thank you for your honest feedback. You're a treasured friend.
- For you, the reader. Thank you for purchasing this book. Know that any profit that would be mine is going back into God's kingdom. Thank you for making that possible. *Don't Forget Me* is a great story for children and a great gift for expectant mothers. I hope you enjoy the story and that you'll share it with others.

Blessings to you,

1 Corinthians 1:3-4

About The Author

Kayla Jarmon is a wife, mother, grandmother, daughter, sister, aunt, cousin, and friend in Christ. When she was a young girl, she wrote poems, but when her eldest son was nervous about beginning kindergarten, she wrote a story hoping to instill a love of learning and of school. As her family read it, they encouraged her to write more stories.

The Lord directed her path to home-schooling when her eldest was in junior high, and she eventually started a blog to encourage and inspire others on the same journey. In the latter season of home-schooling, God directed her path into film making, and she wrote, directed, and produced a feature film with her family. This project awakened Kayla's passion for continued story-telling. She now logs story ideas that come her way and keeps a running list of books, films, and blogs to create while actively working on two to three projects at once.

Kayla recently learned that her grandmother and her parents also loved telling stories. And not surprisingly, her children and grandchildren also love it; she is excited to see how their paths unfold. Having home-schooled her own children, Kayla actively supports the home-schooling of her grandchildren and the home-schooling community at large. She continues writing to encourage and inspire moms, dads, and children to slow down and contemplate God in all things.

Don't Forget Me

Don't Forget Me was inspired when my daughter-in-love was expecting. I asked the Lord if he wanted me to write children's books, and the following morning the idea for *Don't Forget Me* was birthed. This book is my attempt to follow his direction.

Romans 1 says that the ungodly suppress the truth they know about God and exchange it for a lie. And David writes in the Psalms of God knitting children in the womb. The idea for this book sprang from these passages.

Don't Forget Me imagines a conversation between God and Baby in the womb. I hope it causes you to contemplate God as the author and giver of life and stirs you to remember him.

Bump-bumph...

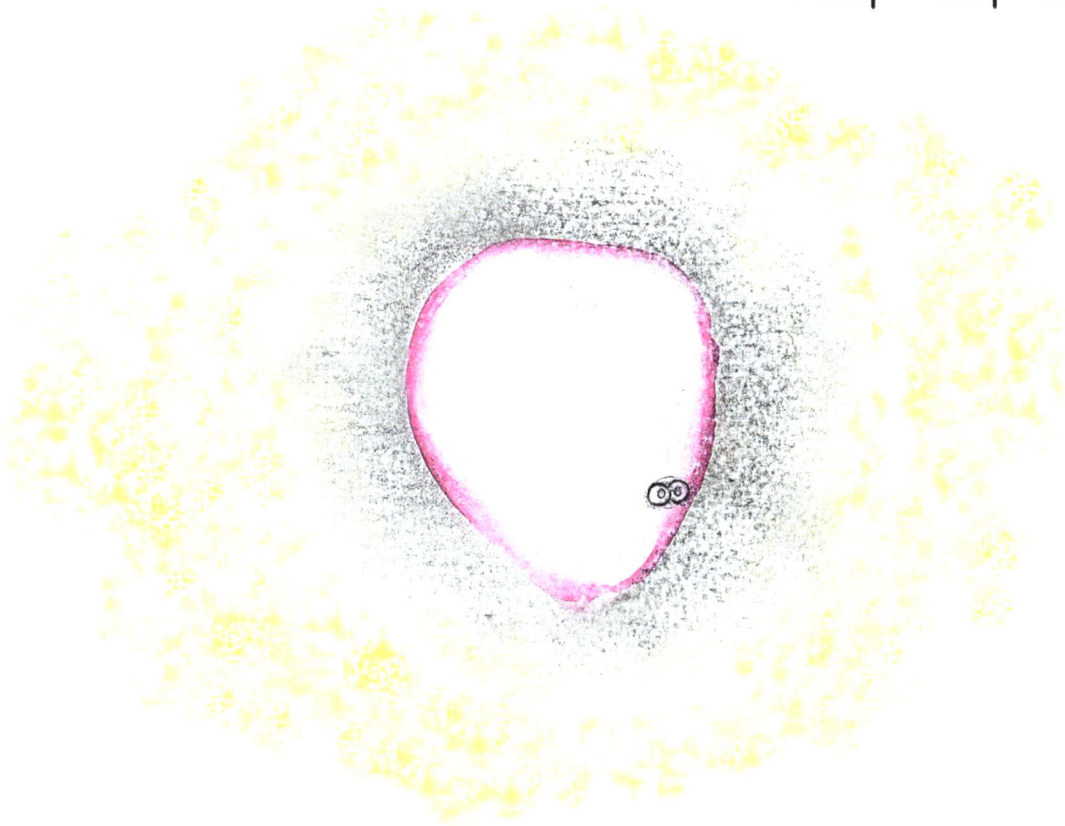

Bump-bumph...

bump-bumph...

bump-bumph...

Bump-bump... bump-bumph...

"Hmm, this is odd...

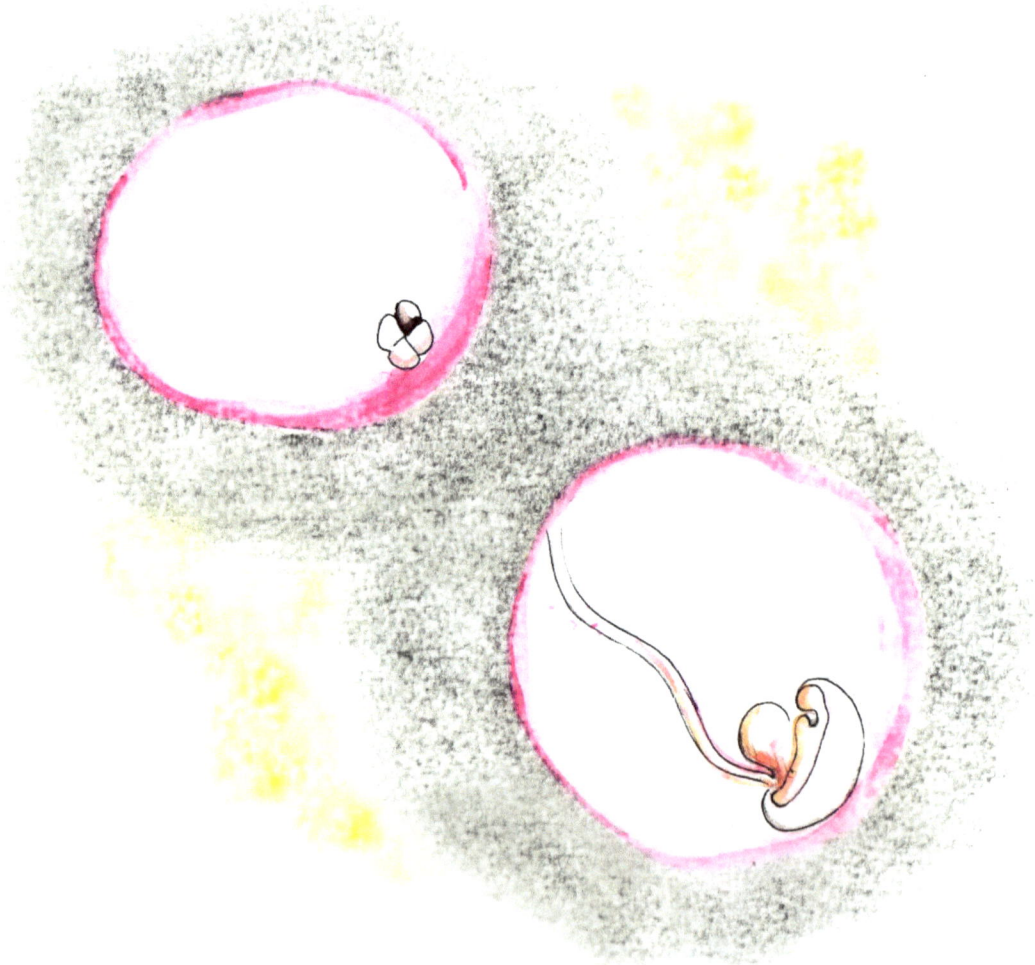

but so warm. Mmmmm, I like it."

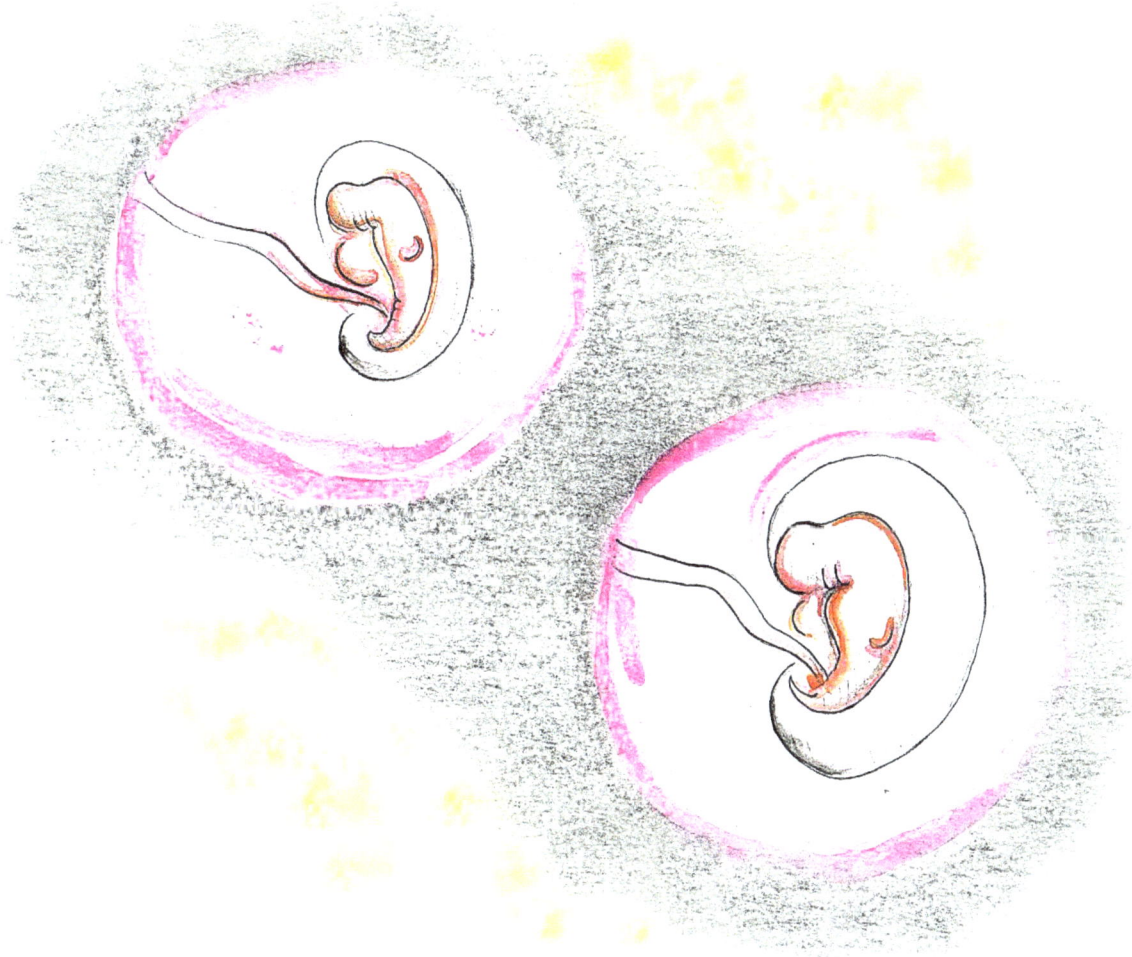

"Remember, I am here."

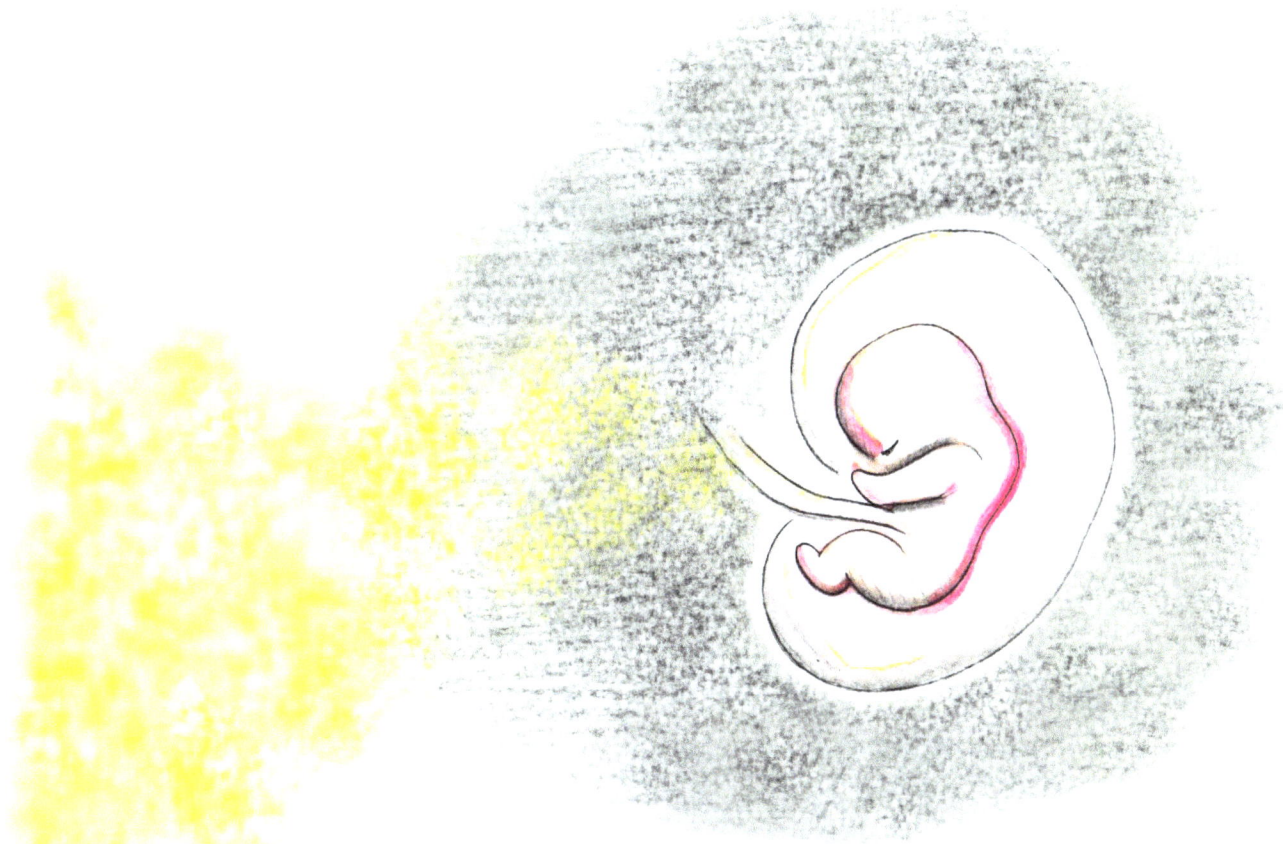

"I'm glad. I like knowing you're here."

"Oh, what's that sound? I feel like I know it."

"She's part of you. She's your mother."

"She's part of me? Oh. She sounds nice."

"*She's laughing.*"

"Oh, I like that!"

"Oooooh... I feel like I'm stretching!"

"You are. It's called growing and
you'll do it for a long time."

"Huh? What's time?"

"Remember, I'm here."

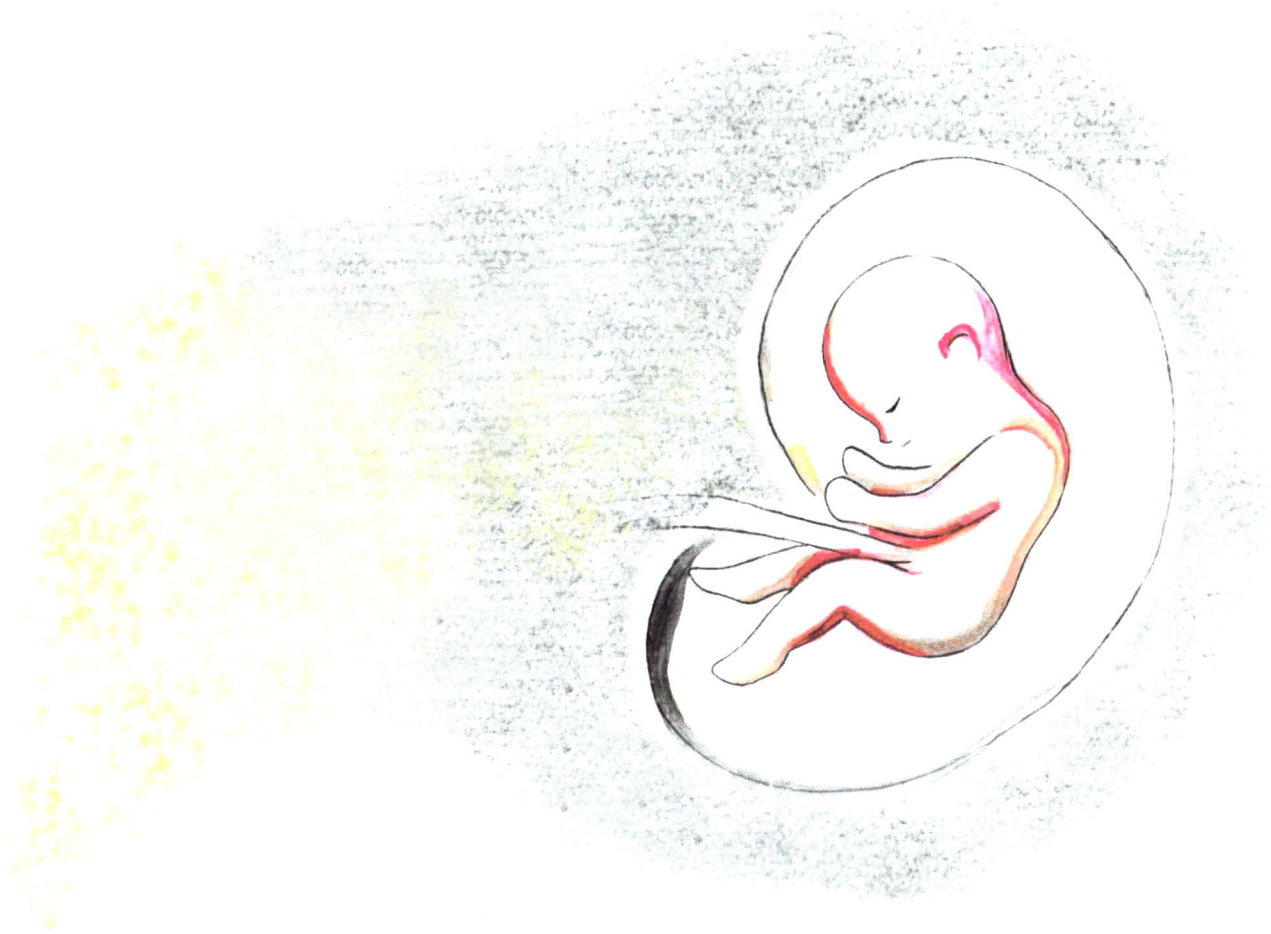

"You already told me that.
I know you're here, and I'm glad."

"What's that sound? I feel like I know it too."

"He's part of you too. He's your father."

"Oh. He sounds nice too."

"Yay! I hear another story coming!
I love when they read to me."

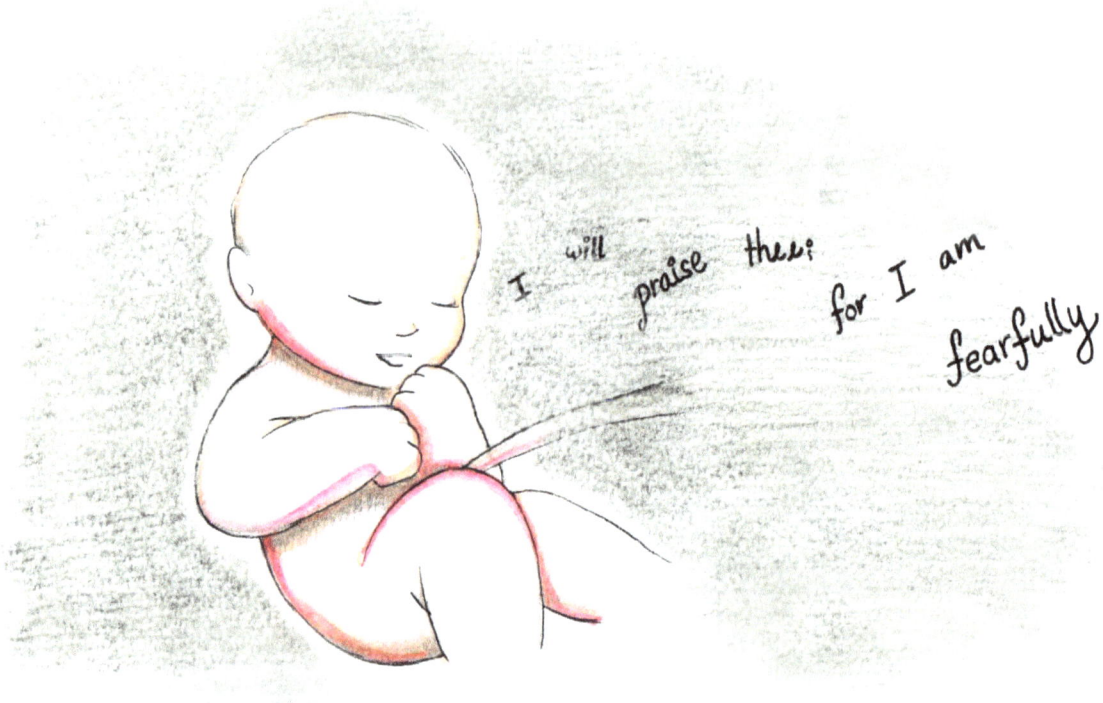

I will praise thee: for I am fearfully

"I like to kick my feet and roll around to let them
know I like it. Will they always read to me?"

"I especially like it when they read your words to me. Do they know about me, like I know about them?"

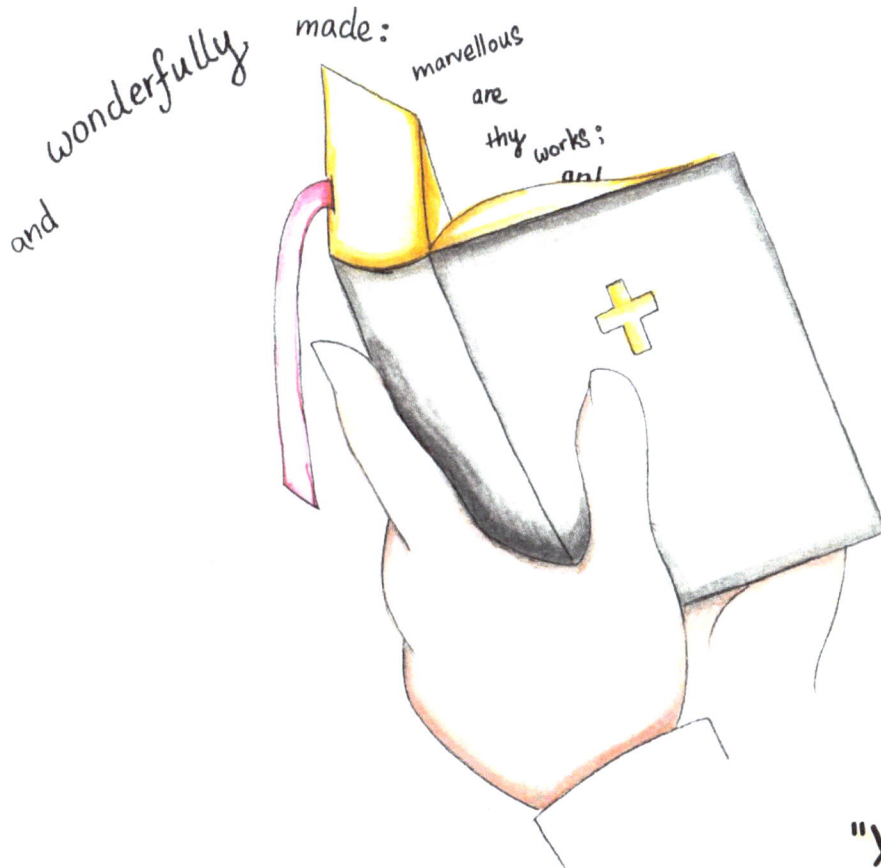

and wonderfully made: marvellous are thy works; an!

"Yes."

"Ugh, my room keeps getting smaller and smaller!"

"You'll grow out of your room soon and be getting a new room."

"Umph, it's so tight. What'll my new room be like?"

"Well, it's being designed just for you, and you'll get to see your parents really soon."

"Good, because I want to see them so badly!"

"Remember, I'm here."

"I know you are. Why do you keep telling me that?
You're always with me!"

"What's that? I don't like that sound!
I don't like it at all!"

"She's crying because she's sad."

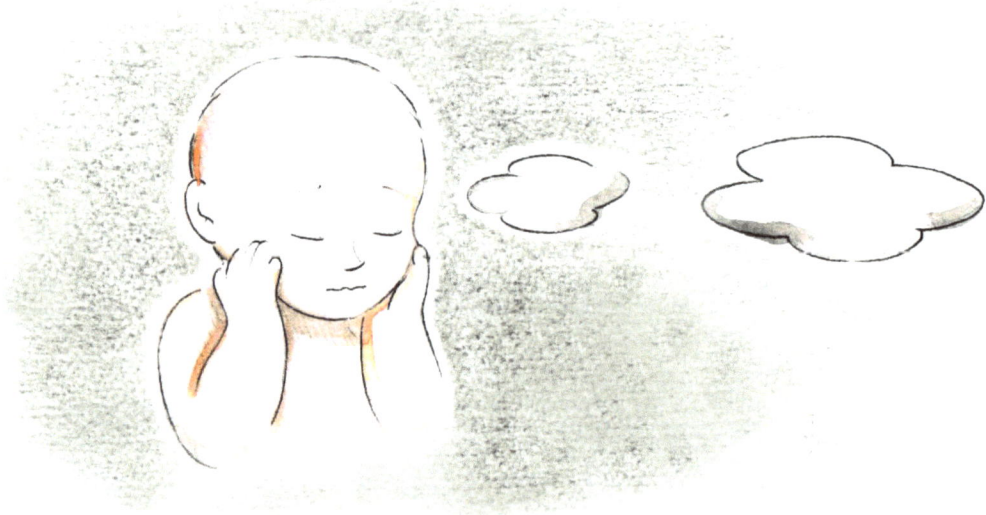

"Can you help her not be sad?
I don't like sad."

"Why not?"

"I don't know; I just don't like it."

"You're learning the difference between good, bad, right, and wrong. It's because of me that you're able to tell the difference. And you know what?"

"What?"

"It's because you know what good is that you don't like her being sad."

"Oh. Well, I know I don't like sad. Will you help her?"

"Oh, good, Father's here. Yessss! He's talking to Mother about you! Listen! She's not crying anymore."

"Hey, they're talking to you now. I love when they talk to you! OK... I'm going to be quiet now because I want you to hear them."

"Do you hear that? She's singing. I like it whenever they sing, and you know what?"

"What?"

"When they sing to you, it makes me all warm inside. Do you like it too?"

"I like it very much."

"Guess what?"

"*What?*"

"They sing to me too! Oh, I so want to see them.
I can't wait to see them."

"I can hardly move around anymore.
When do I get my new room?"

"Soon."

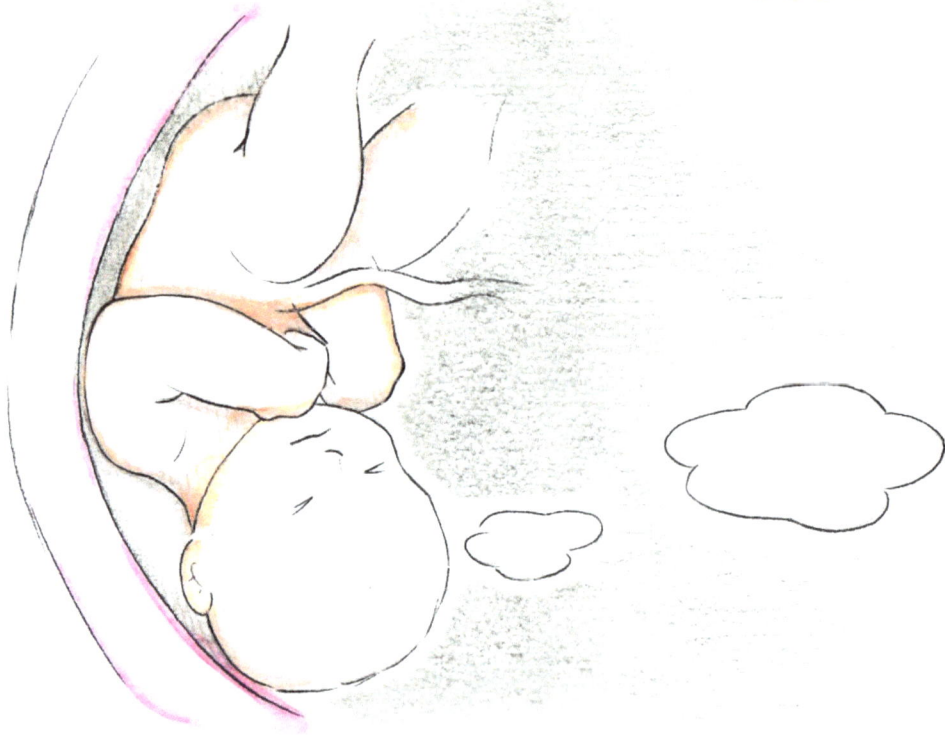

"Good, because I'm growing just like you said,
and it's getting pretty tight in here!"

"Remember..."

"I know, I know. You don't even have to tell
me. You're always here. I know that."

"Here we go again. Why does she get up all night long? We *never* get a good night's sleep anymore!"

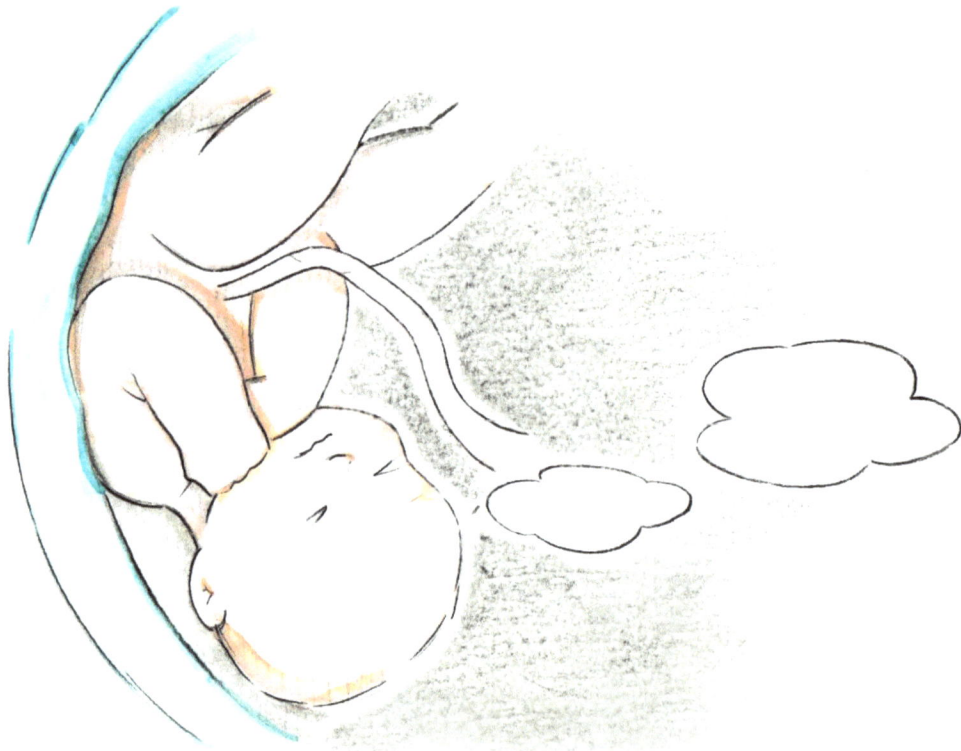

"*Well, it's because of you that she's getting up so much.*"

"What? I'm not doing anything. In fact, she keeps waking me up. How can I make her do anything if I'm asleep?"

"It's because you're growing so much. Her bladder doesn't have much room anymore."

"Uh, what's a bladder?"

"Oww! What was that? That hurt!"

"You're about to get your new room."

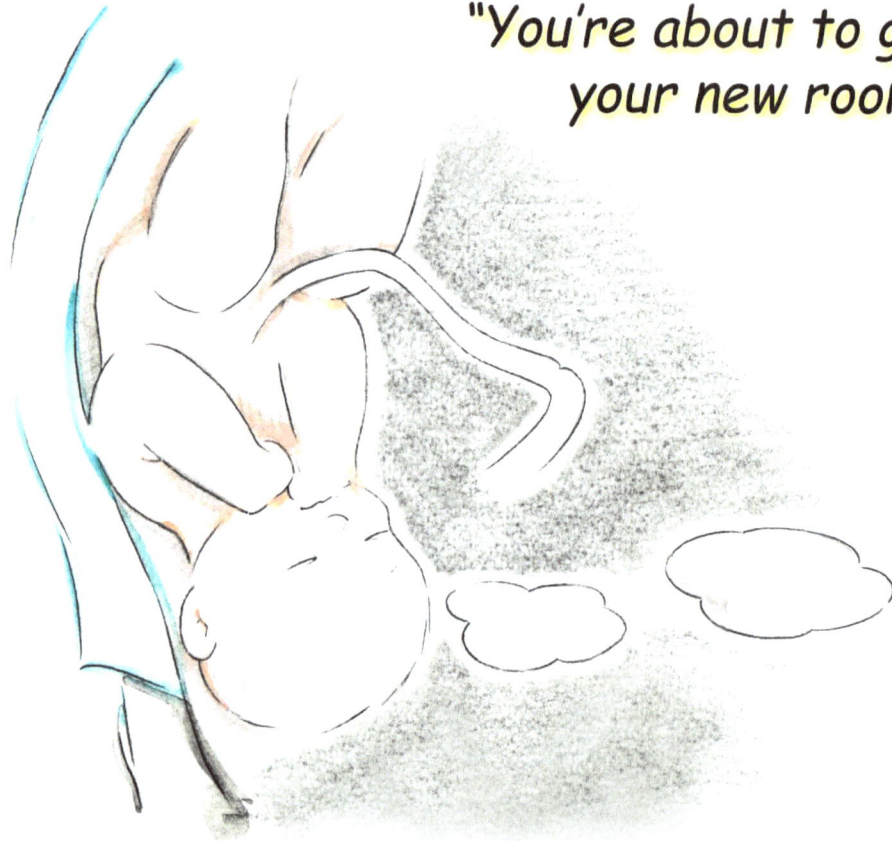

"Oh good! That means I'll see them soon!
Ouch! There it is again!"

"Remember, I'm always here."

"I know you're here. Why do you always tell me that? How could I *not* know that?"

"I don't want you to forget me."

"I could never forget you. Ouch! There it is again! It's getting tighter in here. Owww! Uhhh, could you please make that stop?"

"This pain you and your mother are going through will be worth it when the joy comes. You're going to enter into a world of love that's beyond yourselves."

"Uh, she's hurting too?
            Ow, ow, ow, ow!
                        It's really tight!"

"The joy's coming, and when it comes, neither of you will remember the pain or the sorrow, because the joy will be so great."

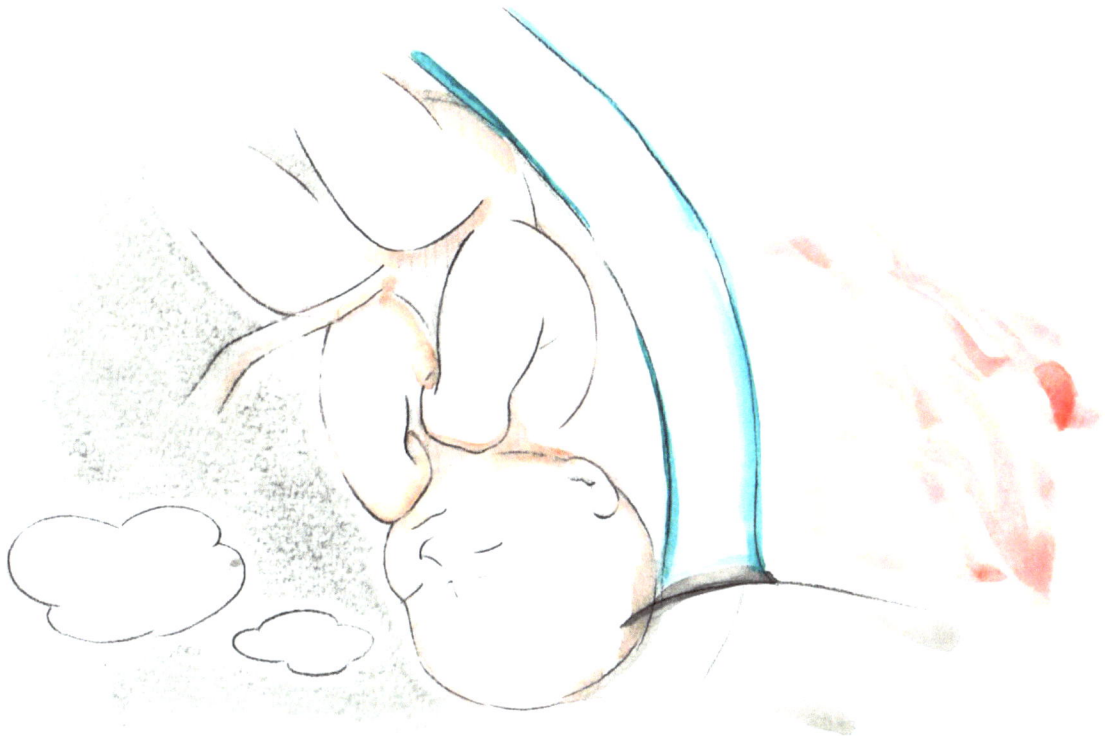

"Ouch!!!! Well, bring on the joy!"

"Who is pushing me?!? And why does it
keep getting tighter?"

"You're about to see them."

"What? Yay! I've been waiting so long for this."

"Don't be afraid."

"What's afraid?"

"You'll find out soon."

"Keep pushing, Mom. Oh my!
Looks like it might be a full head of hair!"

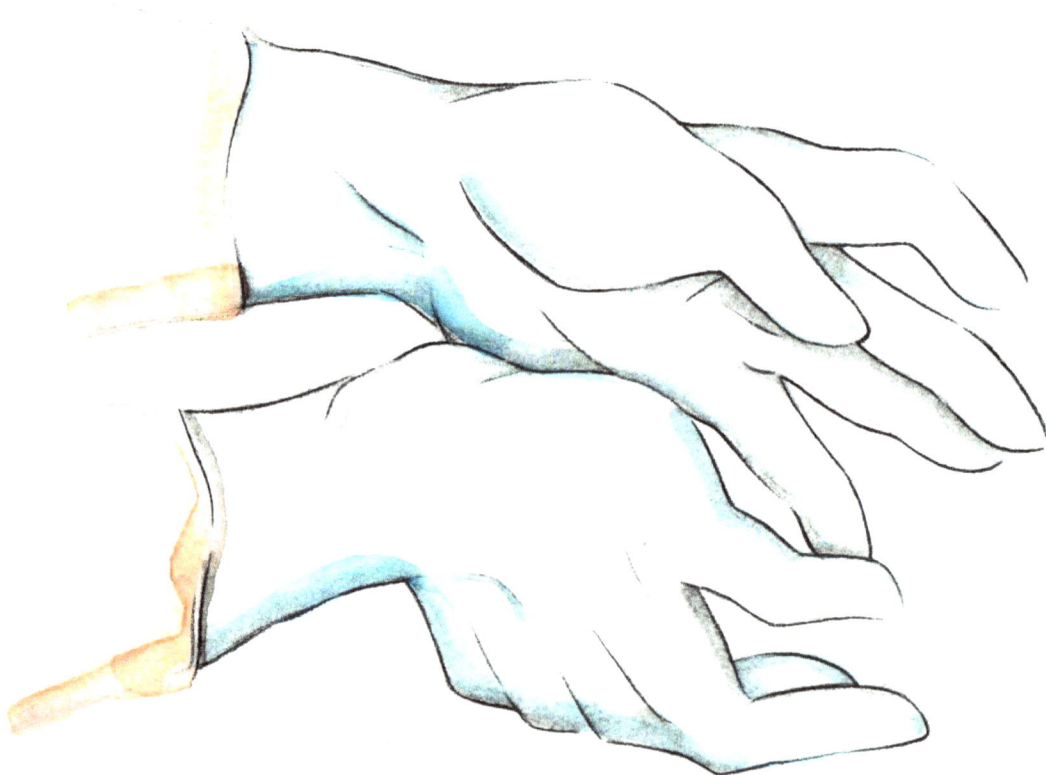

"Who's that? I don't know that voice."

"Remember, don't forget me.
I'm always here."

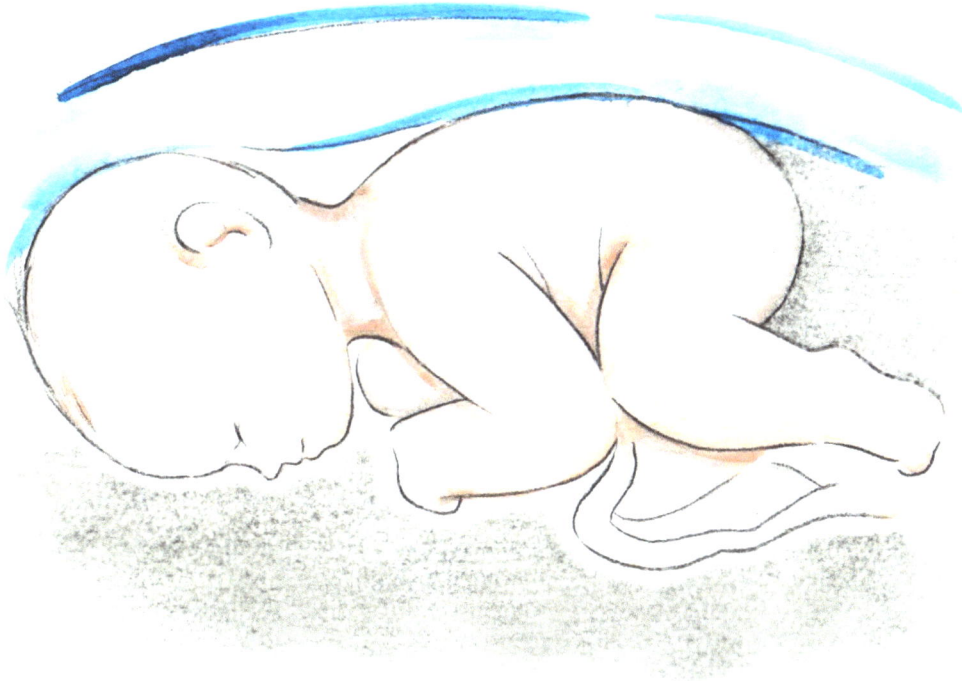

"I'll remember, I'll remember.
Am I getting my new room now?"

"Ouch! I'm a little tired of being pushed and pulled.
Please make it stop!"

"What was that? Did you see that?
It was so bright!"

"Don't forget me."

"I won't. Why do you keep saying that? OUCH!"

"Listen, you've been with me from the beginning, so how could I forget you? Are you going somewhere?"

"No, I'm not."

"Then why do you keep telling me that? OUCH!"

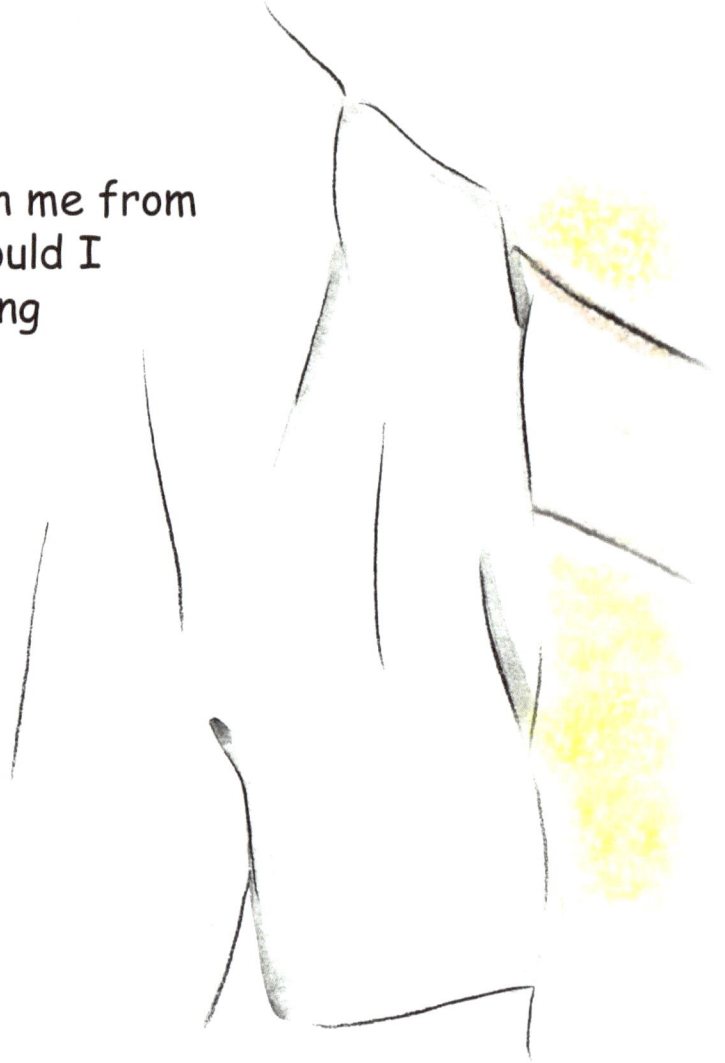

"Forgetting is easy in the world."

"What's the world? You know what? It doesn't matter what the world is; I know I'll never forget you. You made me in my mother's womb, and everything in me knows this!"

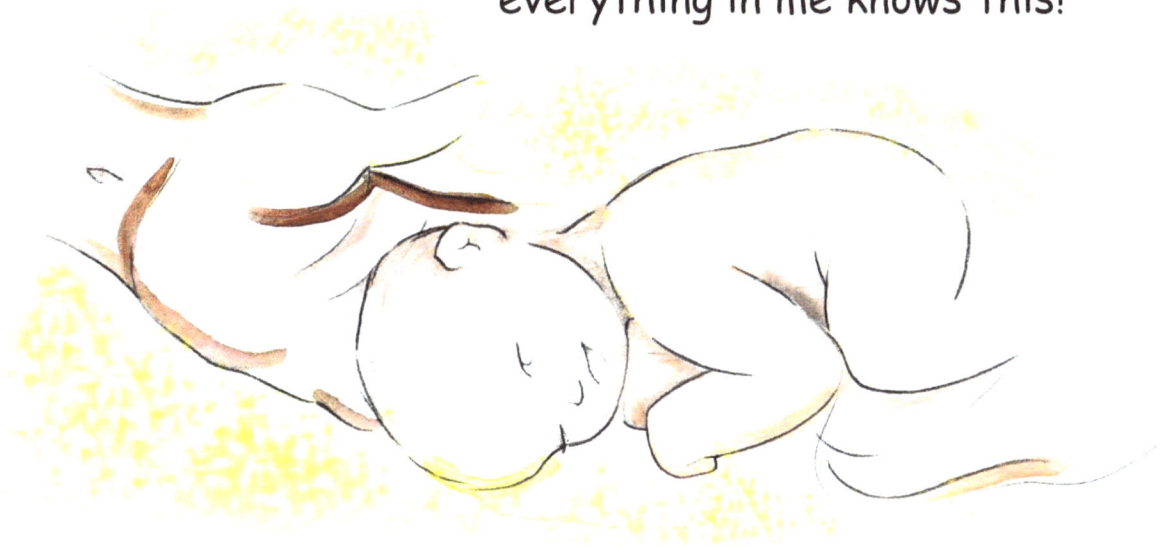

"You even saw me before I was formed, and all the days of my life are written down, even though I still have to live them; so you see, I could never forget you! Never!"

"Know that I'm here and there and will always be."

"Well, I thought you would be!"

"I don't want to share my room with anyone else!"

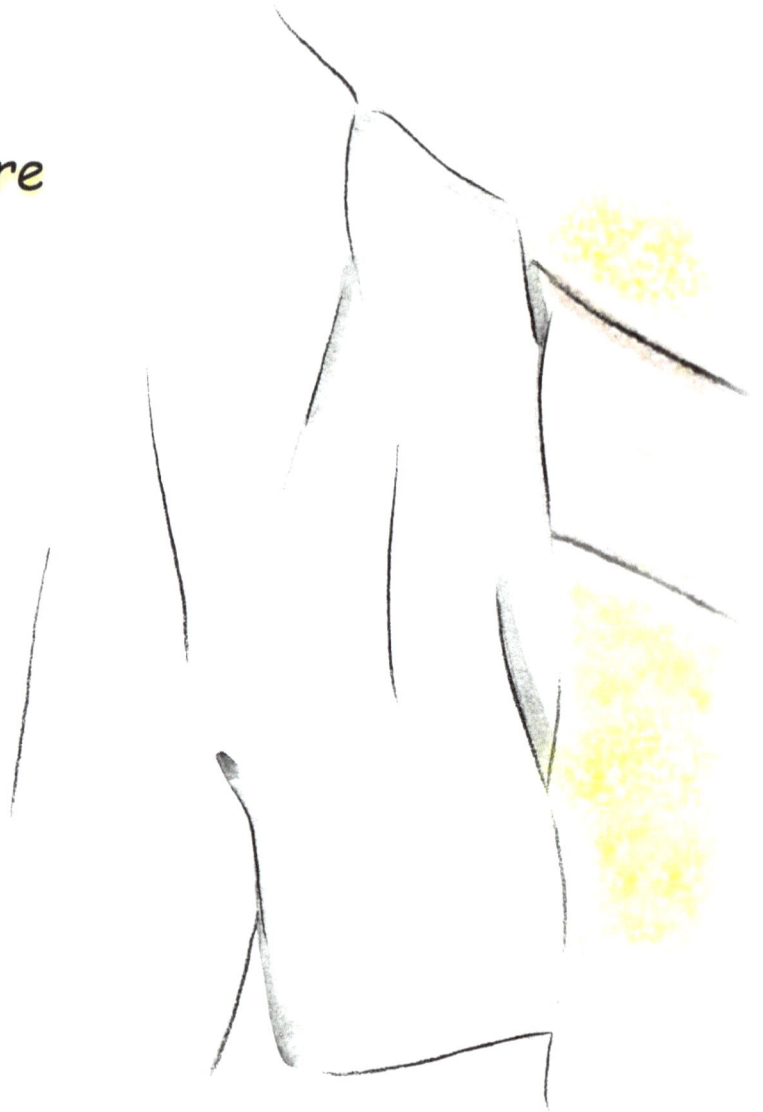

"There's that bright thing again. What is that? It's really bright! Wow, those noises are getting louder too!"

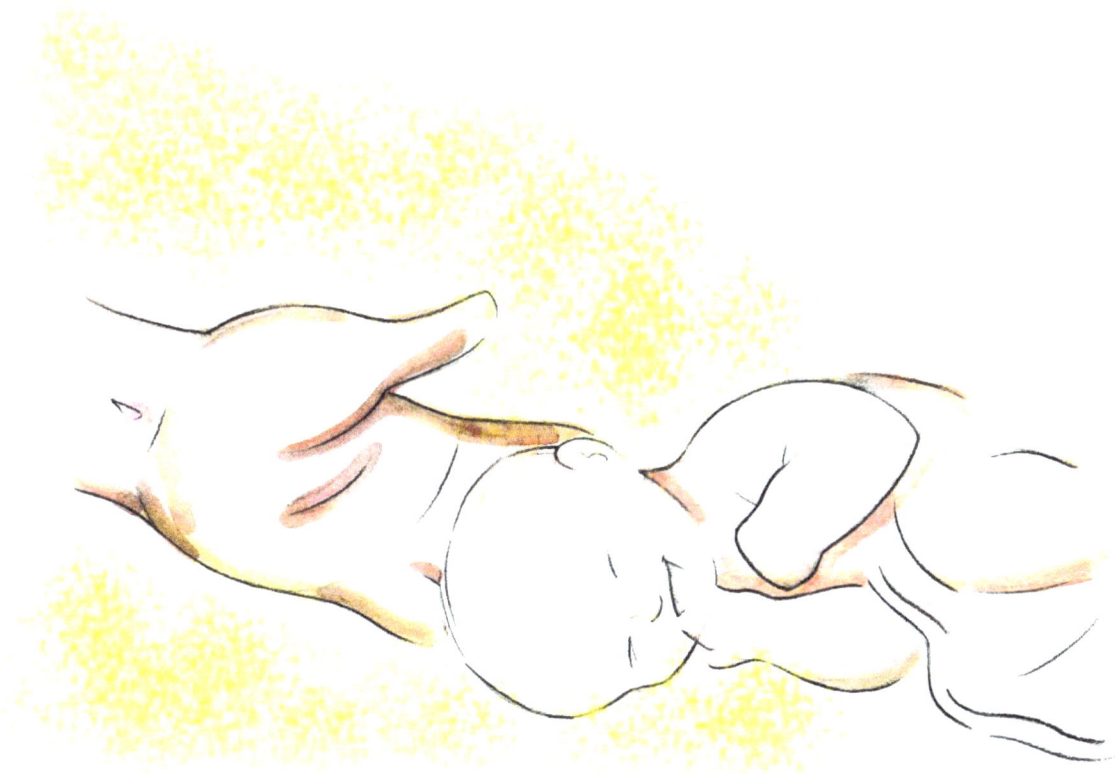

"Don't be afraid. I'm here."

"Mom, just one more push and baby's here. That's it. Oh my! Welcome, you handsome boy!"

"Oooooh! It's not tight anymore! There's so much room! Whoa, there's TOO much room! Where am I? Is this my new room? Bbbburrrr, it's cold in here!"

"OK, here are the scissors, Dad. Cut the cord right here."

"Nice job, Dad. Great job, Mom. Congratulations to you both. Nurse Judy's going to take baby over to the warmer and check him out quickly, bundle him up and bring him right back to you."

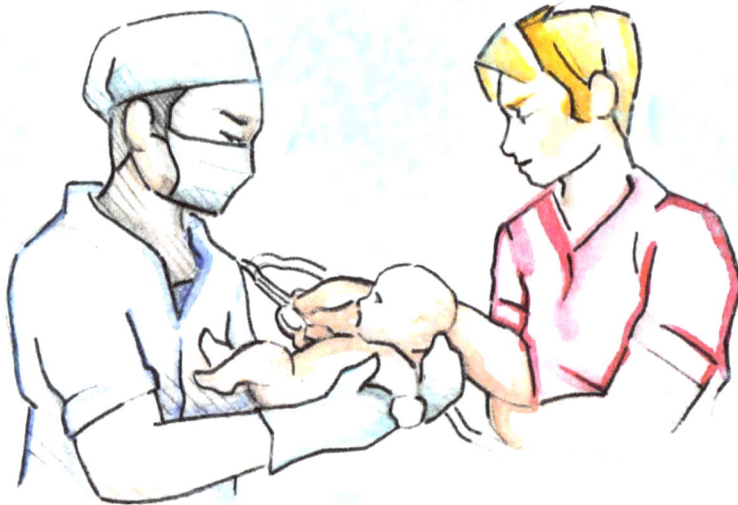

"Thank you, Dr. Carter."

"My pleasure."

"Whoa! It's so BRIGHT and I'm so COLD! Mother, where are you? I'm so cold! Nothing's the same! I'm afraid! Please help me! Everything's so different."

"Oh, it's OK, little guy, but we do love to hear you cry."

"Where's Mother? Where's Father? Whoa, that's bright but really warm. Hey what are you doing?"

"There, there, little man. I'm just listening to your heart and lungs. Nice. Everything sounds good. Mom and Dad, this is one time when we LOVE to hear babies crying."

"It's good for them. He's just getting used to his new surroundings; plus it shows us he's healthy too."

"There, this'll warm you up."

"Oooooh, thank you for wrapping me tightly. This feels nice. But, you're not Mother. Where's Mother? Can I please see her? Where is she? Where are you taking me?"

"Congratulations, you two.
This handsome little guy is all yours."

"Who are you?"

"Hey there, my beautiful, David.
Mommy loves you so much."

"Oh, it's you! It's her! Oh, how I've longed to
see you, Mother! My room is so big!
It's too big! Who's that?"

"Hey, Son. It's so good to see you."

"Oh, it's him! It's Father!
I'm so happy to see you both!"

"God, we thank you..."

"Oh, that's a great idea! Let's talk to him!"

"Shh, shh, shh..."

"Oh, no, it's all right. He can hear us
all at the same time. Really, he can!"

"Hey, little man, did you know God's
the one who gave you to us?"

"We're so thankful.
Let me tell you about our Creator God."

"Oh, yes, please tell me."

"I don't want to forget!"

Scripture References:
 Birth pain and sorrow turned to joy: John 16:21-22
 Made by God: Psalm 71:6; 119:73; 139:13-16;
 Ecclesiastes 11:5
 Created in the womb:
 Psalm 22:9-10; 103:1-5
 119:9-16; 93-94
 **Children are a gift
 from God:** Psalm 127:3

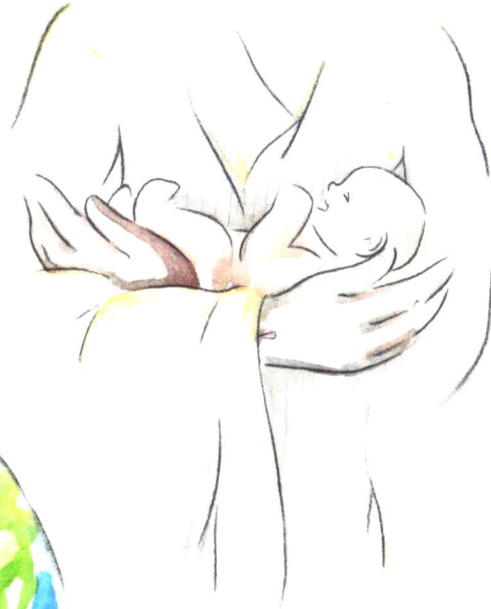

Teach your children:
Deuteronomy 6:4-9
Psalm 78:1-8
Forgetting God:
Deuteronomy 8; 32:18;
Isaiah 17:10

www.ingramcontent.com/pod-product-compliance
Lightning Source LLC
LaVergne TN
LVHW072129070426
835513LV00002B/36